FAUXHAWK

Potentially,

Pain   pain begins with

where   form   code   a   goes the complex

and   event   and the

pain   has evolved a family

cities.   cities overlap

skin, joints, muscle, viscera, bone)   specialized

in vitro,

Our labor   of discrete, internally h

populations

We have used   fluorescent tracers to define the spe

viscera, joints and skin   liminary   populations

required to produce

actual

diverse mechanic

understood, but

BEN DOLLER

FAUXHAWK

Wesleyan University Press
Middletown, Connecticut

www.wesleyan.edu/wespress
© 2015 Ben Doller
All rights reserved
Manufactured in the United States of America
Designed by Mindy Basinger Hill
Typeset in Sina

Wesleyan University Press is a member of the Green Press
Initiative. The paper used in this book meets their minimum
requirement for recycled paper.

The author extends appreciation and grateful acknowledgment
to the editors and staff of the following publications in which
poems from this book appeared, often in different forms and
under alternative titles: *Academy of American Poets Poem of the Day,
Apartment, The Brooklyn Rail, The Boston Review, Fence, Jupiter 88,
Poor Claudia (Phoneme), The LA Telephone Book, Mantis, Textsound:
an Online Audio Publication, Vertebrae,* and *The Volta.*

W. S. Merwin, "Your way," translated from the Crow,
from *Selected Translations 1948–2011.*
Copyright © 2013 by W. S. Merwin.
Reprinted with the permission of The Permissions
Company, Inc., on behalf of Copper Canyon Press,
www.coppercanyonpress.org.

Doller, Ben.
[Poems. Selections]
Fauxhawk / Ben Doller.
     pages   cm. — (Wesleyan poetry series)
ISBN 978-0-8195-7586-9 (cloth : alk. paper) —
ISBN 978-0-8195-7587-6 (ebook)   I. Title.
PS3554.O97428A6 2015
811'.54—dc23   2015020799

5   4   3   2   1

National
Endowment
for the Arts
arts.gov

ART WORKS.

This project is supported in part by an award
from the National Endowment for the Arts.

for Alphabet

Your way
      is turning bad
and nobody but you
      is there

>>

from *Crow Versions,* "Plenty-hawk"

CONTENTS

FAUXHAWK

THE FAUXHAWK

don't go squawk in the forceps shop

go (up) (get born) amok!

rundown your block in a toque or in a flock of spots all tigerlilylike

or just stop giving order

to don't go get shot

you're not and never

will be hawk

rather one of those delicious birds

who chooses walks

I taught I taw tis evening evening's cotillion, thing-
    craft as a comet complex, copper-cropt-cop buzzard, in its sliding
      through the slipstream sonic boom booms the freon-drawn air, and wilding
right there, how it sang upon the scene a careening screaming
in its targeting! Then on, on on it flings
    as its steel hurl rolls hard towards a compound: the remote eyeing
    reset the map-scale. My flesh in writhing
groaned for a drone,—the R/C of, the detachment of the sling!

Bully booty and power and tact, oh, flair, guide, BOOM!, here
    Rubble! AND the pyre that breaks into flame then, a zillion
Times told shinier, more mushroomy, O my musketeer!

    No wonder in it: vaped bods make Cloud-cowed civilian
Ka-Ching, kids disremembered, ah my dear,
    the report cannot be independently verified.

my stooges shirt
my stooge

popular iggy peanut butter
I wear my stooges under work shirts

to stage rage to play
a little ditty to raw power

to passenge alive in
sweatwater bathtops

in heroin hats
the white rats

covered up

half shaved
primate

curing a common
cough

RUN

1

The word is a verb
but the word
is a noun

I noun you
I noun pronounce you
now pronoun you I do—

I am my wife's wife.
I wive. I wave the news at a beetle
who must die.

It runs into and out of
this house
of mine.

2

The verb is a word
but the *verb*
is a noun

I'm deverbing you
I just gerunded

Excuse me.
Words are free
I am not.

The news is good
not so good and terrible,
it runs at least

a hundred
pages old.

3

I run from myself
I am faster this way

I do run myself, oblongata

this sentence
runs on

plant & animal
protein

it ruins the mouthfeel
the best feel

for it feeds as well

I have a secret
I don't know what it isn't.

CYBERMONDAY

\#

flexibleemeralds   spermicidalketchup
petrochemicalbags consistofwhattheycontain

deadscents   sentexpress madeMEDIA
omahasteaksubscription   Foremangrill

testosterone&zeranol droolsthroughthespout
clabberinginthetunacan   fromamazon

arisesthecorrugation   fiberboard ingoosestep
entombing agooselivermaskofaman

Iwillwear   thisrest therestofmylife
Iwilltaketherest ofmylife uponasettee

brandedafter   aspokesmodelcloud

\#

letusnowpray   totheexplicitsentence
theunequivocal inorder tojiveorjibe precise

theprivilegeofpunctuation spitstaintheorder
thecolonoscope   decrieswherewego

isitbadtobeevil   ifsoyouareborn
isiteviltoapostrophize   sacrosanctcenotaphs

it'sjust   Ihavesomany   leftover excretions
it'sthe   justwomanman   rejectstheaveragemanwoman

brandishingan   e-bouquet   HDgeraniums
I'mforgettingtowritesothatImaybreathe

handmethetorch   let'sseewhatthissolventsays

#

nothingforlunch   butfunnylookingdiskettes
nothingfornoon   butfurinasock

themeterisrunning   themeterisrunning
theincorporation   bouncingabucket   onahotday

screwedup   blacktop   plasticsound
nothingbutsun   inplaceofthesupper

businessinfront   carmageddonintheback
themeterisruining   themouthfeel

thepoematablet   protectsyourtongue
it'snicetolookatthemirrorsometimes   thewallbehind

swipingyourcardinastranger'sslot

[EY]

I abase my base.
I abash my bash.
I abate my bait.
I abduct my duct.
I abet my bet.
I abhor my whore.
I abstain my stain.
I abstract my tract.
I abut my butt.
I accede my seed.
I accent my scent.
I acclaim my claim.
I acclimate my climate.
I accompany my company.
I accost my cost.
I account my count.
I accredit my credit.
I accrue my crew.
I acknowledge my knowledge.
I acquire my choir.
I address my dress.
I adhere my here.
I administer my minister.
I admire my mire.
I admit my mitt.
I adore my door.
I advise my vice.
I affirm my firm
I affix my fix.
I afford my Ford.
I affront my front.
I allow my low.
I amass my mass.
I ambush my bush.

I analyze my lies.
I anchor my core.
I appeal my peel.
I append my end.
I apply my ply.
I appoint my point.
I apportion my portion.
I appose my pose.
I appraise my praise.
I apprise my prize.
I archive my chive.
I arrange my range.
I arrest my rest.
I ashame my shame.
I asperse my purse.
I assault my salt.
I assign my sign.
I atomize my mys.
I atone my tone.
I attack my tack.
I attest my test.
I attire my tire.
I augment my meant.
I avail my veil.
I avoid my void.
I avow my vow.
I await my wait.
I awake my wake.

LACANIAN INC.

aw hell I am
at a such a great
distance from

this conflict
in the halfawake
uninvolvement

I couldn't even
pretend to read,
see, I have

amassed this
massive inaccessible
intelligence, better,

knowledge, eminently
translatable in
vocab-sense yet

the syntax
I consider hostile
as it I cannot

occupy, like
walking on a historical
flood—THE—

westernspeaking
(what starts the west up?),
where the guy put

the beastcouples
on the boat, all aboard
the mythosphere,

right?, & what
about all the lonesome
creatures, what about

the poor wet plants?
God was god
mean. Now

we have the imperceptible
cloud, but remember
when your hard-

drive crashed
& all you had
was, like, blasted

into the nowhere
from which
Already this thing

is exhausting, the mere
weak endeavor alone:
packaged in this eyeball

trimeter whatever,
if I were you
I wouldn't have

come this far. Maybe
bathysphere would
have been funnier.

Should it instruct
or delight. Brrr.
I'm a little chilly—

let's do this
in the sun. Not
bad, though I have

to squint. So that
shall be my platinum
leash. And that

shall make me free
to articulate my business
in a practicable manner.

All I am
is early into
the obviousness

of my 3rd trimester,
squinting, autobio-
graphically. Wouldn't it

be nicer to upgrade
the interface?
A lighter legtop?

Artists like apples
because they restrict
creativity, thus allowing

more. Can't beat that.
Give me small
holes to blow through.

Also, the matter of the sexy
titanium compact. The matter
of matter being "sexy."

The matter we call matter
but is not what is the matter
with what is. I am

not an artist, I
just like to type.
Kidney dialysis/dream analysis.

Urges, negations,
substitutions:
One word

    for another: that is
    the formula
    for the metaphor,

        but I prefer failure
        in all its
        dangling

            permanent permutations,
            prefer saltwater
            to water, the way

      it goes liable
      for life, yet it cannot
      solve this global

    drought. Yet it cannot
    solve its steady rise,
    the effacement of all

  beyond taxonomy.
  I prefer it molecularly,

this H_2O, this NaCl,
not the drought itself,

  not what this human
  blood has done & does do.

There go those thirties, not in making,
but in consuming the reappropriation
of Indonesian plywood embossed

with the Swedish flag. Shout it out: a passable
enterprise, we enjoyed it, flat-packed
for the premier and only tick of relocation +

ultimately crammed in a context unununlike.
Sometimes a system completes a subsequent
system. Sometimes you need a triple negative

to persist. Mostly dead language is all
you get to get. I don't think I can hack
it tomorrow. How to ship my model ship

to you, how? Look at this having + what
more: the will to be had. Look at this this,
redescribe the current potential, flaking

as it is pronounced incompatibly. Sausage
Queens of the Inland Empire. The casings
shellac cuz intestines R gross. Frankenstein

clomped so Edgar Winter could Keytar
an albino hailstorm. Frankenstein yowled
a way to tell Percy Bysshe he die. I select

the veneer that most accurately reflects
my inner fleshtone. And strip the screws
that make it cabinet. And strip the screws

that make it close. And turn the thing not
to be turned. And build a bag of sawdust
headweight. And nail the nonincluded nails.

And graft and graft to appendage 17. And
swallow the screws when the neighbors
are occupado. And abridge the instructions

with a hearty heehaw. And heft the lith
with a herniated heave. And join the jaw
with woodglue and wait. And sand the joint

with the shell of a snail. And where the hell
do I get the snail. And practice is this modular
obsolescence. And fashion a shelf to hold itself.

AXE BODY SPRAY

we the people
assaulting trees
of the other sex
pheremonal ladders
of retinal plastic
boom out the roots
we like ourselves

beast on the proscenium
screen or mallet spike
the split gets heard
in your hands gets
blood on your dust
milked malt balloon
eye jam on the jammies
strike nowhere

we the peephole
survey says
earth googleplex
calliberationist lib
I the ascender
practicing military time
at a checkout line
strike somewhere

checkout my sheckler
she hates good things
precolonial ballroom
prancercise and prototype
apples never to crunch
the sun tm takeout
the papers and the trash
she hates this bikini
my manmade man eyes

o skewered birds of film stock
I overlined one entry on nature
from the many versions
thus was peace strung

extremely bright even
highlit blinding evening
amusing eventually
among the shams
technocracy and the adds

much later sold a pun
to get me to go away
I could do this for a living I alleged outloud
as long as I'm awake

revolution is repetition
I bore my friends so
I hate my love
handle a DVD
taught myself to
fight myself
already inside
papaya mechanique

IRONY&ARCHERY

Live together
in perfect ha
rm money side
by side on my
laptop keybo
red oh lord w
hi don't we d
o it in the r
ode? Archery

hits the spot
occasionally,
less often at
an amateur
level. Irony,
alternatively,
offers the ad
vantage of an
indeterminate
yet twin targ

[BEE]

I babble my bull.
I baby my bye.

I backbite my bite.
I backdate my date.

I background my ground.
I backlist my list.

I backtalk my talk.
I backwash my wash.

I badmouth my mouth.
I badtalk my talk.

I bamboo my boo.
I bandage my age.

I baptize my ties.
I barrack my rack.

I bartend my end.
I bedeck my deck.

I befriend my friend.
I begin my gin.

I begrudge my grudge.
I beguile my guile.

I behead my head.
I bemuse my muse.

I berate my rate.
I besmirch my merch.

I betray my tray.
I bewitch my witch.

I bisect my sect.
I blackball my ball.

I blacklist my list.
I blindside my side.

I bogart my art.
I bombard my bard.

I bootleg my leg.
I boink my ink.

I boycott my cot.
I broadcast my cast.

I broaden my den.
I brutalize my lies.

I buffer my fur.
I bureaucratize my ties.

I butterfly my fly.
I buttonhole my hole.

whiter I make it when walking right in
unswerved, sweating fluorescent bleach,
preaching a moon page that says its welts:
learn this by heart is empty but do it
to do it. I make it somehow whiter, zombied
and I opified allover the absolutely
whitest room. I say keep your lines in line
and look at me now just lining them,
some flogged orthodoxen, ploughed
down sillion shiny sacerdotal lines
I'm supposed to like and looky I do.
I like what I like. I just like what I like.
I like to say look: dissident anachronistics,
shambolic stuff in master rows but look
at me. I even early balded to enhance
the interrogation. I meander in and form more
order. I like to point with my pointer, to
indicate. The most afraid I like to get is
a little bit. I app my accounts and survey
the advantage. I tower under.
I oxiclean the ivory. I shower and shower.
I dig on fonts. I wake up singing I say
never start with that but one morning
I wake up singing the Fat Boys. I wikipede
The Fat Boys. One of them is no longer.
The other is no longer fat. I assess the Human
beatbox via a Schwittersian optic.
I exercise my massive rights. I have the right
to remain. I remain. I interview just
like a glacier. I hand dance. I like just
what I like. My skin is white not. It fits
just tight. It burns on will. My horizon
is fungible. My will is like whatever.
My SPF is infinity. People seem to like
me. I was just born just this way.

POLYNOMIAL POETRY

I drink
more coffee
than anyone
in my apartment

I get by
on more sleep
than anyone
in my department

<< insert tree name here >>
<< play with etymology >>

any thing
is below my grade
if images were less
deadly I'd put one here

I didn't have
heart to say fascist
boots on the ground
and coffee aren't images

<< something mythological >>
<< something biological >>

I like technology
but wouldn't marry me
I like paper too always have

eat it like big
league chew I like you too
I get to tell you what to do: read
on because the page instructs you to

<< ink to the scene in Jurassic Park
where the T-REX chases the car >>
<< MIRROR the MIRROR >>
<< play THE SLIDER >>
<< try the sliders >>

NEUROBIOLOGICAL POETRY

Neurobiology hasn't destroyed our life. Hence,
it's made this all possible. Nonetheless,
renal damage accompanies any aperture.
We are beyond finding rhythm in the beyond,
taking serious time. Evolution evokes
into the false festival of our cocktail.
Take ourselves, please. We pay fines for the books:
history, misogyny, mythology, neurobiology,
synonyms anonymous, interest itself
tazes us into objecthood. Shall we do
day? Half an epiphany? Do a bad job at
our bad jobs? Or all of the above,
but halfwary. Or, all of the beyond.
Inventions intimidate us around
the corners of the World
Trade Center, two of these memory
ribs. And, in the ear, the Pacific,
where the greatest linebacker
ever rifles through his chest
with a flashlight, preserving
the brain for silence,
droning that may
be a drone drone
this is another
concrete poem
look it
ends
in
I.

UMBILLICALL

operating from a feeble
exposition

no navel no link no
landline nor arm

wrestling the land
lock condominimum

decisive swashletter writ
in handmedown

spout smartcarnage
aged just white

holy whateveready
corresponder you choose

who wrings the action
from the auction nearby

it is just a wiry way
to talk into

a kind of unkind (naturally)
troll awaits (of course)

to toll the wayfare
audit an addition

nailed the fuzzy rack up
to get reception in

series where whatever's severed
creeps on

[SEE]

I cache my ache.
I cage my age.
I calendar my lender.

I caliper my leper.
I callous my loss.
I camera my era.

I campaign my pain.
I curate my rate.
I canker my anchor.

I cannibal my ball.
I canoodle my noodle.
I capacitate my acetate.

I cape my ape.
I capsize my size.
I cash my ash.

I castrate my trait.
I celebrate my rate.
I charm my arm.

I chart my art.
I chauffeur my fur.
I cheer my ear.

I chip my hip.
I chloroform my form.
I chronicle my call.

I cinch my inch.
I circumcise my size.
I clap my lap.

I click my lick.
I climb my limb.
I clinch my inch.

I clip my lip.
I cloak my oak.
I clog my log.

I clone my own.
I clot my lot.
I clover my lover.

I cluster my luster.
I coil my oil.
I combust my bust.

I compass my ass.
I conserve my serve.
I conceal my seal.

I confront my front.
I craft my raft.
I control my troll.

I crap my rap.
I cram my ram.
I crash my rash.

I compile my pile.
I compost my post.
I consult my salt.

I concede my seed.
I console my soul.
I consult my salt.

I compromise my promise.
I comprehend my end.
I cancel my cell.

DUMMY

Isn't it dumb
to write a

letter
at a time.

The noisy
dummy says

nothing funny.
The assembly

doubles up.
The drummer

drops her
dead gum.

Isn't it dumb
to say that

one is an
atomic

fact. The hand
of a man

mum in
a maw only

the curtain
conducts.

OBVIOUSLY

The curtain is kind

of cool. Hitchcock
liked it. Why

not. Great place

for getting shot
or famous or for

bleeding back

behind the iron
one. The score

diegetic as they

come. Bernard
Herrmann forever

human.

The gowns hanged
in greenroom ligature.

Edith Head never

dead. Great place
for a nail-bomb.

A cold one.

Watch them watch
their watches run

out of wick.

Obviously this opera
sort of sucks

you in or off

your seat. You
see phony fire

and roar it too.

THE FOREIGN CORRESPONDENT

psycho therapy psycho
therapy psycho therapy

spare me the trinity
I myself and me

we wouldn't batter a bug
abdomen thorax head

I like takin' Tuinal
like Arthur Koestler et al

double suicide has never appealed to me...

of course
in the course
of the course
of the tale
the course slits

however, I cannot live without Arthur, despite certain inner resources...

it takes x-large violence
to gore the wood

to fit in the fire
to bang a spy

it takes an x-deep dredge
to dredge this

b&w bog

EARING

knocks drags shells
because

drugs lines clothes
should've

pimple span pricks, tickles
gaps and then

gaps standin in for
hot what

I don't have get ready
You is earing me out

Insert every [1]
where 'con [2]

tempt' for 'a [3]
ttempt,' that [4]

is, garage [5]
door lurch, [6]

steep heat [7]
lost, teeth [8]

can't chip [9]
the lung [10]

ellipse once [11]
the sentence [12]

is begun: [13]
it takes [14]

just one [15]
(word, blurt) [16]

to detest [17]
the gap [18]

you say—[19]
I mean [20]

I say— [21]
to hate [22]

the way [23]
it never [24]

works. Well,[25]
'hate' may [26]

be too [27]
strong a [28]

word. More [29]
the disease [30]

of speed[31]
on black[32]

ice. The[33]
unease you[34]

know will[35]
kill you.[36]

I'm meaning[37]
me. Hello[38]

I say [39]
though it [40]

seems far [41]
a way [42]

a sort [43]
of hell [44]

gleams, fades,[45]
and waits.[46]

1. Hello: The poem functions in the book as a phatic and in media res greeting as well as a belated introduction to certain poetic effects and themes that are mobilized throughout the material. "Hello" is an Americanized compromise selected over the course of millennia from a multiplicity of alternatives: "holla" (stop, cease), "halon," "holon" (to fetch), and many more, hunting hollers ("halloo!") and hailings. Each term conveys more a sense of pulling another into one's sphere than an act of politesse or acknowledgment, an interruption or imperative as opposed to an introduction. Hail Caesar. Sieg Heil. Hey Girl. Halt your motion and attend to your addresser. Not until Edison successfully lobbied that the word be used as a greeting for telephone calls, a way to acknowledge the scratchy silence about to be breached, was the term standardized. The telephone was originally envisioned as an open line between two offices, and a bell was originally proposed as the way to initiate a conversation until Edison's suggestion ("I don't think we shall need a call bell as Hello! can be heard 10 to 20 feet away. What do you think?"). Another Bell, Alexander Graham, who is credited with the invention of the telephone, but who appropriated much of the vital technology (including a liquid transmitter) from one Elisha Gray, argued for "Ahoy!"

2. Insert every/where: As in proofreading, word-processing—specifically, Microsoft Word for Mac 2011, version 14.2.1. The reference is intended to signal the poem as linguistic material, as is the enhanced enjambment at the end of this line and subsequent lines throughout. This prosodic mechanism was "inserted" after numerous drafts, including one loosely attempted in the sonnet form, which in a weak and impoverished moment somewhere in the shadow of the US economic collapse of 2008 was composed and submitted in hopes of procuring a $20,000 National Endowment of the Arts grant for poetry writing. Indeed, many zones of the poem (now de-sonneted, reformed) still reveal the writer's desire to yield to a faceless, empowered, entrenched, and fundamentalist poetry referee (see the ghost rhymes, the clunky dramatic volta still perceptible near the end of the poem, the empty silhouette of "discovery" and "the writer" the writer has not yet been able excise). Nevertheless, it may be observed that the anxiety inherent in this compromise with an imagined governmental audience and this extraordinary violation of aesthetic ideals is embodied throughout the passage of the poem: the spluttering shame apparent at the very notion of naming anything at all.

3. The only line of more than two words tactically contains a word and two halves. Tempt: to try, make trial of, put to the test or proof, to try the quality, worth or truth of —OED.

4. Repeating "tempt" in so short a space generates additional scrutiny towards the connotations therein: temptation and its role in the Pandora effect of articulation. This broken echo simultaneously amplifies more distant, yet appropriate associations: seduction, crime, and even murder. One of more than one instance in the poem where the staccato line and vertical syntactic velocity places physical pressure on the idiomatic semaphore of kinetic conversational bewilderment.

5. The mouth is a garage for storing one's body.

6. Our personal physiologies may well relate to the types of diction we are drawn to as individuals, especially in the case of verbs. In this case, the writer—being of the taller yet constantly chagrinned type, carrying himself awkwardly and hunched throughout his lengthening life with no small

consequence to his spine and nervous system (not to mention the organs that rely upon these synapses to operate accurately), practically incapable of holding a glass of water or an opinion without spilling it on the thirsty earth below—tends to employ verbs like "lurch."

7. In public performance this portion of the poem can be a mouthful to articulate (what isn't?): contented form in the sense of simulating the difficulty the poem is speaking of and to. Sound it out yourself, slowly. "Steep" here (slang) refers to the high price of fossil fuels used to alter the temperature of one's home as the temperature of the earth changes as the result of human beings and their attendant industries cremating these same fuels.

8. Despite the levels of revision and reclamation the poem has suffered, one still pauses at this point, wondering if perhaps all punctuation should be jettisoned. Or perhaps the entire piece should be obliterated save the couplet:

Steep heat
lost teeth

9. However, one hopes that the inclusion of the comma (one breath unit) between "lost" and "teeth" subliminally transmits the stilted rush of binary, unpunctuated enjambments that follow, as well as the residual violent descriptive energy accessed by placing "teeth" and "chip" atop each other, a sort of belated field effect where one word is tinted retinally by another despite being unconnected in terms of direct syntactical connotation, as "chip" clearly refers to

10. the lung

11. ellipse

of intention that is impossible to disrupt once verbalization is instigated. Here we move from 10 straight monosyllables to two disyllabic words in a single couplet, this surfeit mouthstuff anchored firmly to the twin concepts "ellipse" carries: the unbroken ovoid chain and the indirect, oblique statement. The big o.

12. A life sentence, of course.

13. "Has begun" is an acceptable variant. The manifestation of the colon in poetic context, the inside out and the out in.

14. It takes and takes and takes.

15. "It's true that what is morbid is highly valued today, / and so you may think that I am only joking / or that I've devised just one more means / of praising Art with the help of irony. // [...] The purpose of poetry is to remind us / how difficult it is to remain just one person, / for our house is open, there are no keys in the doors, / and invisible guests come in and out at will." —Czesław Miłosz

16. The manifestation of the parenthesis in poetic context, the capture and the clasp. The cordon and the clutch. The word blurt.

17. "Test," "Tempt," and "Text" are only a few letters apart. They are also utterly synonymous.

18. Feel free to think of the clothing store, or mind whichever gap you have in mind

19. as this is the 2nd person portion of the poem, the well-kept common grounds where the reader provides the sandwiches, wrapped in the news. Here however, the voice in the poem lurches, the subjectivity staggers, manifestation of the em dash in poetic context, word with an invisible self inside itself, interruption by way of explanation, aside inside, plus and minus and always another (line 21) to come, expectation and obliteration, segmented foil to the lung ellipse, the only binaries we know: R U—oo—II (Dickinson)?

20. The partition between reader and writer shrivels but only for the duration of one line, as authority is regained, as Identity is recaptured, as meaning is reasserted, as the poem is snapped back into its lyric duty, back to the mean, the median medium who speaks only for itself. Subject and subjectivity merge, delivering a more lucrative and familiar poem-surface.

21. Poetry makes the private public. Poetry makes the public private. Poetry makes the universal personal. Poetry makes the personal universal.

Poetry makes the political apolitical. Poetry makes the apolitical political. Poetry makes control out of chaos. Poetry makes chaos out of control. Poetry makes the word a word. Poetry makes a word the word. Poetry makes nothing happen. Nothing makes poetry happen.

22. "Contempt," "detest," and "hate" constitute 3 of the 92 words in this poem.

23. The exact midpoint of the poem. 6 of the 46 lines in this poem rhyme with may.

24. Poetry defines the indefinite.

25. Note the possibilities for dual, yet complimentary readings of this line, had the poem been presented without punctuation (see note 8). This effect should be noticeable in public (or private) performance, given an excruciatingly slow reading or recitation, complete with full two-breath enjambments.

26. Single quotation mark vs. italics for the purposes of isolating the word itself. Infestation of the citation. Scare-quote with a single finger. Scare-quote with a middle finger. Curved back towards the head itself. Devil locks.

27. Clearly a homopun on "be two" as well as a rhyme with "Me/You": both obviously demonstrate the plasticity of the subjective skein. 1733 SWIFT Impossible! It can't be me. Or may be I mistook the word.

28. Both the articles "a" and "the" conclude lines in this poem—self-consciously signifying either the amateur status of the poet (the only rule in poetry being not to end a line on an article), or the poet's insistence that every word (blurt) of the construction is equally significant to the whole. Every word in this piece occupies an optically empowered position (either at the beginning or end of a line) except for "for" (line 3) whose significance is promoted by this anomaly.

29. The most inspirational single line of the composition.

30. Funny story, the nouns "disease" and "unease" (line 34) were swapped in a late draft, trading in the synthetic comfort of emblematic exchange for slight surprise. Note the apocalyptic dismissal of—yet complicity in—a language system that can only express via false equivalences.

31. The vehicle released from the metaphorical garage.

32. Note the numerical parallel with the previous line.

33. "Black ice": actually, a thin glaze of transparent ice over a dark material such as, in this case, asphalt.

34. Anxiety, being, of course, the nucleus of any poetics. All poems being demonstrations of no more than their cellular limits.

35. A play on the 'better the devil you know' axiom.

36. Stage 3 cutaneous malignant melanoma.

37. (nothing should ever begin this way, so much already does, though it does have a kind of candor, it does establish a scope, a sieve, a slot to see through, a sieve to see through, though these items are all too worn [tut tut], I shall have to avoid them altogether, employ [hmm] the figurative only as an expansive device [well], a means to disturb the surface rather than to refine or clarify, and 'I' does have going for it one thing, at least, it stands right up there don't it, all line all the time, divining rod, lonesome, singular, and ironically subtle [subtly ironic?], thin intimate [pardon the compound modifiers, the condomsound] confession precursor whisperer [pardon the piling on], perhaps the figurative should always provide a figure and if this is writing then figures are scriptures, absolutely not the holy version, but as in scrawlings calcified to print or whatever this font is I'm typing in right now [Cambria, somehow], scriptures, pre-print though I hope someday this will be printed, that's the point I suppose, it could go in my bio-bibliography which will be sent the Council, it could help them keep me, or rather me keep them as I am the disposable entity here, discipline and publish, though what if it is digitized, when is it, what is it, I am aiming for an extreme kind of candor here, it cannot be clarity as Oppen wants it [so it says on the poster facing the toilet] because anxiety runs as muddy [ouch] as that pacific I've

been trying to play in lately since I live nearby, since it is summertime
and since it is too cold the rest of the time to really get in, a kind of candor
I've noticed I am uneasy with, and so I notice each of these clauses covers
another which is part of the thing, the figure on which if you skate you will
eventually scratch a trench) apostrophe m(what a choice, you lose a verb
compounding yourself, expunging an action [am, though?—not so mobile]
while twisting the self into a process, which it is, admittedly, but is writing
an act of fixing [in the sense of making definite, in time and place], or
braiding while unbraiding)me+an(medium median who speaks only for
itself, only through approximation, through addition and then division, and
then selection, with the remainder rounded one way or an other)ing(kinesis
mimises, braining while unbraining)

38. Me, an aim I call myself. Additionally, the first appearance of the
titleword—a popular and effective tactic that capitalizes on satiating low
expectations.

39. Note the reorientation into linear subjectivity, the pure present tense,
the proclamation blooming into a shameful and totalizing singularity. The
tectonic shift between me and I. The final couplet of a sonnet once launched
here, its corpse still identifiable, though disassembled, undone. Poetry, alien
autopsy.

40. "Though" marks the most nauseating turn in this poem, gathering
itself, as it does, for a kind of thesis-making, puffing hard a nothing word
in rehearsed formulation of a manufactured epiphany. Although, the word
has been used successfully by Donne.

41. see ms sees me messy seams

42. Word bisected for spatial, dramatic and sonic effect, as well as the
hope that this rupture, however small, may distract somewhat from the
sentimentality of, if not the statement, then its shape.

43. Following two lines originating in "a's" should be read simultaneously
as the pronunciation spelling "a" as in "sorta." Only an acute anxiety of
suffering the label of gimmickry (though the writer professes an affection
for gimmicks, gadgets, gizmos, and games) has prevented this selection.

44. "Miss Stein laughed and said 'hell, oh hell, hell, objects are made to be consumed like cakes, books, people'" —"Tender Buttons," *New Yorker*, Talk of the Town feature, Oct. 13, 1934

45.–46. "Let's grant that poetry, because of the primary role played by rhyme in creating its enchantment, has, in its evolution up to our time, proved to be intermittent: for a time it gleams, then fades and waits. Extinct, or rather worn threadbare by repetition. Does the need to write poetry, in response to a variety of circumstances, now mean, after one of those periodical orgiastic excesses of almost a century comparable only to the Renaissance, that the time has come for shadows and cooler temperatures? Not at all! It means that the gleam continues, though changes. The recasting, a process normally kept hidden, is taking place in public by means of delicious approximations." —Stéphane Mallarmé, Crise de Vers

PAIN

Titles are but nicknames, and every
nickname is a title.

>>

He lives immured within the Bastille of a word.

>>

Society in every state is a blessing, but
Government, even in its best state, is but a
necessary evil; in its worst state an intolerable
one: for when we suffer, or are exposed to the
same miseries BY A GOVERNMENT, which
we might expect in a country WITHOUT
GOVERNMENT, our calamity is heightened
by reflecting that we furnish the means
by which we suffer.

>>

Thom Pain

A) Objectives/Tasks/Concept. Recent advances in directed energy weapons technology suggests that scalable, non-lethal to lethal force systems may be possible. Such a system would be useful in many environments. Two systems currently under development, active denial and pulsed energy (ADS and PEP) offer mainly complementary capacities that could address multiple tasks. These tasks include the ████████

Consider   thee   carefully

The full capability of these directed energy systems (DE) are still being explored. At their current stage of development, each system has clear non-lethal (ADS) and lethal (PEP) capacities suitable to the above tasks. Our experiments will examine the feasibility of PEP as a new generation non-lethal weapon. Pulsed energy can be configured to produce plasmas of exceptionally high energy.

that generous fluorescence pain

In the studies described below we will determine the feasibility of using the plasma derived EMP to induce pain suitable to disarm and deter individuals or form barriers to the movement of large hostile groups. If successfully deployed, PEP could complement ADS in situations in which the latter is ineffective, less effective, or prone to countermeasures. Many of the countermeasures that might be envisioned against ADS consider the more it seems we offer opportunities for PEP targeting (via plasma induction or ablation of the defense). Despite these potential advantages, certain special capabilities and features of ADS offer advantages over PEP in many scenarios. Therefore, the systems are complementary.

The efficiency and lethality of PEP weapons systems are straightforward. The non-ballistic, instantaneous properties of DE make precise targeting a straightforward matter of line of sight. Terrific amounts of energy can be delivered over great distances with pinpoint accuracy. However, ████████. Potentially, the application of PEP

talk it the deeper pressure bottom sounds we talk
blow the candle
it makes it terrific the time the rise to state & statue heat per inch
worst to live   skinny viscous   nerver   like tombs we break everytime
                          ending

The pain induced would be relatively instantaneous, and the duration of pain would be limited to the duration of application ████ insider ████ perfectlywell the wooden way Taser-like motor effects are also possible, although these are not investigated in this proposal.

In a separate application, we have proposed studies to quantify the ████ characteristics of laser induced plasmas created us the space saved   the swollen vantage   with micro-, nano- pico- and femtosecond lasers of multiple designs and capacities   detachment   new periods of pain
bubble the mouth owes   These studies will examine the characteristics of ████. In the studies described below, we will describe investigations that explore the human effects of LIP. Studies are proposed to determine the capacity of ████ pain to evoke pain. These studies will be performed, *in vitro*, where the factors such as distance and orientation can be tightly controlled, and where the appropriate pain system components can be isolated for detailed quantitative study. A portion of the investigations will apply ████ to sensory cell preparations. These ████ will be generated by conventional means. Subsequent studies will use laser-induced plasmas to create ████ that element ████, the characteristics of which will be well defined ████ the blank ████ and optimized to produce atraumatic sensory influences.

Objective 1: To determine the features a wanna cry **that activate nociceptors and the extent to which this activation is effective without trauma.** Pain is a primary component of all NLW. Pain can distract and deter individuals resulting in voluntary immobilization and/or flight. Nociceptors are the fundamental detection component of the pain system. Nociceptors transduce a variety of stimuli (gated ionic current) and then encode the pain signal (action potentials). While the mechanisms are not fully understood, ADS operates mainly on the *transduction* component by heating biological tissue to activate heat transducing proteins at a sub-traumatic level (B. Cooper, Microwave Techniques for Stimulation of Nociceptors, NTIC proposal, October, 2003). In contrast, ████ 19 syllables old ████ could activate nociceptors at the level of

Consider thee carefully

    what thou taketh for pain

consider the care

    underwater eking half-breaths
    through a marshstraw
                hid from howling hounds who have

considered thy every

    item: the sharkskin shawl
    the seahorse suit thy forgotten hand
              and have

considered an image so fine of thee

    thou cannot reach it it is for dogs only
    it fits their meat   it finds the line
    made mire   then the line made
    muck   it pulls the gunners nearer
              the torchmen & torturers
                    bayonetteers
                    barometers

Bog   go

their handfuls of wet stones

into thy surface serious.

eke a breath   it is just now spring
eke a breath   there is an ice to it

consider thee carefully

what is pain   is an ice to it
just now   just now the evening lip enters
thy cattail   what is spring

ice turning

unhinge the eye   what
unhinge your eyes   the colors yellower the waves more
                                 brown clouds the hounds stomp out
                                 out fire minnows & silvers

consider their voices you drink them down

  there and *where*   consider—
        what hast'ou done

for what become game?

        for a gaze
         of a gaze
          gave back

for an occupation
in the brush
assembling pain

for a considerable glee

a dormancy

consider ye carefully

take pain:

midless, pure rive, all coast,

plane where one hot drip would be the world,
planet born dying in a day that does not revolve,

coast of matter & other,

lidless eye blind by
handheld fire

and this is pleasure
consider ye

pleasure
the other fire

He lives immured within the Bastille of a word.

She sieves coiffured within the phone bill of a word.

He drives brochured within the painpill of a word.

She graves censured within the good will of a word.

He dives coutered within the flour mill of a word.

She wives Saussured within the firedrill of a word.

consider   careful

for there are helpers who care
         to help, perfect volunteers
paid pointing twigs it seems

where they perceiveth'ou
         to be, considering oil it seems
for they bring oil in a barrel

it seems for they break a barrel
         four hurl it in
rather on for all parts settle

in the middle for it is the taller
         part of the eyeball
then four more broken barrels

go *bog* (they must have a cart)
         minnows and silvers
fire into thee their soft metal

then at thy feet they flee
         o it is nighttime then
til the torchmen unfurl

that ancientest flag of men
         o it is daytime again
then day in its very yellow

solar daughter chopping finger
         o it is time   perception
complex & upper

encoding, thereby bypassing the transduction level. Induction at the encoding level is potentially more advantageous, as it avoids the direct heating of tissue and the risk that occurs from this time dependent event. Moreover, by engaging the encoding event, ███████████ will not rely solely on specialized transduction proteins that are selectively expressed in a subpopulation of sensory afferents. Although they differ in isoform and distribution, the proteins that mediate encoding are present in all excitable tissue. In objective 1, we will determine the influence ███████████ on nociceptor activation, focusing specifically on cutaneous nociceptors that innervate superficial skin (epidermis) and underlying tissue (dermis). The ████ strength required to induce activation, the contribution of pulse duration and burst frequency will be defined in tightly controlled experiments, *in vitro*. These data should prove to be very useful in interpreting the potential human effects of LIP, and its potential as a NLW.

Objective 2: **To examine the influence of** ███████████ **laser plasmas, on nociceptor activation and determine the extent to which this activation is effective without trauma.** Completion of objective 1 will enable a set of hypotheses that will guide studies of objective 2. With an understanding of the 'safe' parameter range for ███████████ ███████████, directed choices can be made to study particular laser ███████ configurations on nociceptors. Using identical recording methods (but laser stimulation) we will examine the nociceptor activating properties of laser ███████████ ███████████ configuration and stimulation regimes.

level threshold to tolerance level	waterline consider ye the greater
excruciates they wreck the level	to take the level up the stationary
wheel moves sound but I am	analgesia myself not an around
to endure but it is punishment	enough distant and later acute
and chronic flashes in the way	every element the day in the wheel
level roll shooting sharp besides	one eye is cold birth comparing
the unprepared to the trained	at present we must be content
with schematics in lieu of exits	there is another manner of matter
examples include the genius "sun"	a severe percentage level score it
a day again another and a weld you	learned the concept when you
learned the word you most of all	sum of all interstellar space
which includes most other matters	sprays of hurt so fine, no

the labor we delight in physics pain

B) Background

Laser Plasma Technology. There is increasing interest in the use of lasers for non-conventional defense applications. This is not only a consequence of the recent heightened sensitivities in such areas as homeland security, defense force protection, and law enforcement, but it also comes from new technical opportunities becoming available through the increasing pace of developments in laser technology. Developments in solid state laser technology in particular are leading these advances. Diode-pumping, for instance, for the first time enables electrical pump energy to be selectively channeled to specific laser transitions within solid-state laser media, leading to vast improvements in laser efficiency, compactness and stability. New evolutions in laser architecture, like fiber-lasers, slab-laser amplifiers, active phase control and ultra-short pulse technology are rapidly opening up new parameter space in sciences and technologies having possible relevance to new defense applications. One of these areas is the field of laser plasmas.

amphibians fasten your windholes
                    lilysmoke   sunshine   eke thy breath
                    herons phoenix up your bellies full
                    springtime   pupil boils thy windpipe
                    has an ash   thy marshstraw   blow glas

consider thy pain

                        chug frogsong
                        glug gaggongs
                        gamalons go
                        bog go

down & under

under & downer

consider cold

    is it pain it is administered to take pain away
   but it is pain   ice turning   just a spring
                turning
                to a coil

    there is a certain numbing   the thawed hurt hurts

    is it pain   makes thou other than other than another
       say, a pond

              it is

    say a pond & it is   then say   pain
    pain there comes a sort of smile   pain
    a grimace I guess   we wring   pain
    from a pond
          but thou art not another thing
    from thy pain   silvers fly from it herons

    or is it light

        which moves

birches torches   freeze   just   as well

just   ice sizzle in a well

o breathing o is not saying anything

adjust yourself

but to call outloud to drown

& live

this jury agrees

underpain of desertion
underpain of blanketlessness
underpain of dying
underpain of lonely

underpain of death
underpain of gnashes
underpain of sourgut
underpain of succulence

underpain of one the dream
underpain of pain
underpain of embarrassment
underpain of praying

underpain of nakedness
underpain of barricade morning
underpain of pill after morning
underpain of husk whips

underpain of itchy finger
underpain of fish
underpain of iron
underpain of siderolite

underpain of branding
underpain of brand
underpain of supercollision
underpain of composition

smashes the sandgrains
underpain of againy
underpain of pathway
underpain of pans

underpain of punishment
underpain of prong
underpain of Pan
underpain of filthiness
underpain of prominence
, underpain of penance
underpain of listening party
underpain of underwater

underpain of grid
underpain of previous grid
underpain of asymmetrical exercise
underpain of ye
underpain of Wrecking Crew

underpain of dolly
underpain of that exact window
underpain of water
underpain of over and over the crow cries uncover the cornfield

underpain of play
underpain of justice
underpain without injury
underpain of sidewheel birth

underpain of tures
underpain of purge
underpain of dry bread
underpain of windows

underpain of 28 degrees
underpain of pain
underpain of how modern
pain of underpain.

consider, once (so so often it is told), in the way
what was can be

that precise treetop
showing all you could hold

in your face which was all that was seen
half the country, century

sentry all you could hold you could have then
green birds with white heads

crime adorable crimes

an inch up offered a mile out
so you inched so high it began to bend

tried your saliva
on the hour

seemed a hand a horn a holler
what was best then

consider that projectile noise

how good was it that
what divined divided

how good was that
land to be born

others were available
books unbearable books

silent books

allday ye
to consider ye

in the finished bird
the dagger of the gun

the severe feather, singsong
needle taking pain

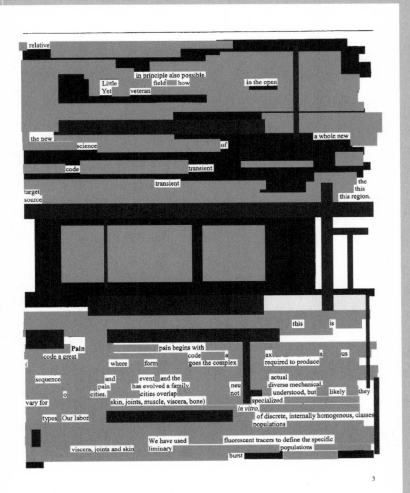

relative

in principle also possible
Little   field   how   in the open
Yet   veteran

the new   a whole new
          science   of

          code   transient

                        transient   the
                                                                     this
target   this region.
source

                                                  this   is

          Pain   pain begins with
code a great   code   a   ax   a   us
                  where   form   goes the complex   required to produce

    sequence   and   event   and the   actual
                    pain   has evolved a family   diverse mechanical.
        o   cities.   cities overlap   neu   understood, but   likely   they
                    skin, joints, muscle, viscera, bone)   not   specialized
vary for   *In vitro,*
                                                          of discrete, internally homogenous, classes
    types   Our labor   populations

                              We have used   fluorescent tracers to define the specific
          viscera, joints and skin   liminary   populations
                                                  burst

3

burst bear one thing to make
a sound thing

hear hear it is
one thing
to make a thing
to make it easy
another to make a thing
to change a thing

I wouldn't change a thing
the ideal curtains
have been achieved
I know precisely
what it is I mean

to do. This contemplation
belongs now
this expression of the curtains
of the stove
broiling beast.

Thereforego intentions correspond to our set.
I am preheated. A buzzer
has it

wouldn't change a thing
not the ironic district instance just
what the which
doctor implied.

Not the scale, not the view from here to here.

GOOGLE DRIVE

If someone is alone reading my poems,
I hope it would be like reading someone's notebook.
A record. Of a place, beauty, difficulty.
A familiar daily struggle.

>>

Fanny Howe

The noon just made it today
As the drone guy gets reamed
By the Republicans

Perfect weather pierces the universe
In the city that disproves the climate plot

If I stop working, I'll sleep better
Since the work I click to the cloud
Like being dead but circulating

Noonlight on Bruce Nauman
Finished middleclass and no neon sins
Til the sundowns

But repetition makes another an other
You whose last customer collages her evals

I'm rewriting Fanny's book probably a gift for a friend
Or from her file I stole it from the faculty lounge

My office is her office, maybe,
No one had opened it yet

On Google Drive, the eucalyptus trees
sing Philip Levine

behind the Korean
bakesales.

And I'm paid to complain
I don't like the way this kid is arranged

on the page, "No one knows who I am."
Some Macs don't get hacked, the elevator

gave all the staff cancer,
significantly lowering morale.

Each cluster's head will gorge inside
a burst of a colon, wet breast or head.

In this carcinoma, literature
and munitions,

a malignant testament. I couldn't write it
as you wrote it and make it what you

must have meant, so on I went.

Blackbird stealth fighters sure make noise
Mach 12 over beachvolleyball totally Top Gun
Officehours are over, but there's a Spanish Miltonist
Interviewing for an empty chair, holy smokes

The weather so soft I go vegan for the challenge
Hunger as an element, not hunger,
inconvenience as continuous present

You just know the daughters
Skyjacked the text

Paradise Lost, if these wars are my Vietnam
Oh Fanny I've barely watched
So no thanks
Hold the onions, shouldn't you be on strike
You've been working since you made me my grassjuice

Three hundred and twenty seven more days
Are due this year and even with that many lives

I'd still be this lazy

Unlike myself you are immune to cliché.
Yours is faith to write what you say

myself, I can't always tell when I'm joking
and I pop out of bed plotting paths to get loaded.

In a 19th century Spanish play, in quintillas,
Milton moves, writes, & ends up (almost) dead
but not before he blesses his child

to wed his chief rival / friend he adored
but not before he took down the Lord

in metaphorical regicide. Plays are things
we put on to occupy the kids.

Another historic blizzard in Boston
Where all the history is
In Washington they can't get a background check through

Some kind of supercop copkiller
Casts from Hollywood, his manifesto so hot
Traffic goes glacial at the border

The LAPD hasn't changed since Rodney King
if you're going to buy a pair of pants make them tight
enough that everyone will wanna go to bed

You can't even measure the snow total
It whips around like the zooms
Blood diamond drills

The loneliest girl in the whole damn town
A rough sketch of a good sketch
Smack in the epicenter the news is creaming about

Word, sentence, word, sentence, word, line, word

A partitioned public segments demonstrations
therapy fluffies help too.

Up Google Drive a solar path sings on
LEDs on a boulder bear where lunch is consumed

commonspace for collective flatulence.
But down that path a car
learns to steer itself same way I steer,

eyes at ten and two—scuttle to the shuttle
back to the medical center, back again,

a hundred earbuds arranged unphased,
50 smartphones swyped full of racist vernacular

and a billion jingles permitted to shuffle.

Hate poems, in the name of language
To be restrained in the core of the sun
A shitload of shit

Every other other is available
Skipping through the lasertag of the TJ margin

Balanced ambivalence is good for the core
So what pigeons step from their stone ledge

Idly munch the weather you ordered
Vacation pills for all entrepreneurs
Subtlety the suntan

Ignore Capital's memory and not your love
Later—if you're a good client—
You'll sleep safe like a man on his gun

Even after you have awoken
You who are for anything that jerks on your nerves

You check the box, I check the box
Bing-ing fertilizer in the marine layer

These poems are my taxes I write
Everything off even the security door I purchased
To signify children and death

It's mostly gravy, hoodie and boots
You in your pronoun you haven't unpacked
Another cardboard clamshell

So let's donate the donuts
We couldn't ingest to the veterans

We admire. Just get a receipt, history
Swigged a faceful of ink

Begging, I admit it, I needed a drink
Well, I feel I hopped over a racecar

It's always the middle of the clock
When sharks play it straight, a peccadillo
in bridge, as in bridge-bombing.

Sometimes I outsource identity to you device
For the good of society
Fondle my reflection in your operating system
Check the humidity. Phonetic pleasure

Of a million million forbidden fruits, trochaic
trachea bridle I choose your compound heads

Intimacy kits can't sheath the application
From the interface. Weep on the window
And wipe with a microfiber stocking

Expensive success. Luxury tax
We all have our little cyborg glitches

I just want you to tell me where
everyone needs to eat, open now, 3 or less $ signs

Meantime you've writhed out of your cracked cover
Revealing your birthmark inscription

Designed in California. Assembled in China.
Schizophrenia is hearing voices, not doing them.

Being raised near the nuclear plant spoiled me
For cheap sunsets and beautiful power
Ditto LSD and LOL, all shriek electron
Loss.

It takes great genius to exploit stereotypes for profit,
The only art is transparency failure,

Whatever that is.

But what wilt thou, body, do
To deploy my body again?

Please please like like some colors—
The flesh against the anthill—
Body by Monsanto.

The wind blew bills from a chainmail bag
Every currency in circulation
Doing the ghost.

My job made page work wage work
alien stepchild. He weaves Ethernet

all day, it's highly unethical.
A concept fails

only in incompletion
in its undone (predacted prenditioned)

dark geography
one inconceivable conception?

Addicted to abandon sounds, signs.
You want to be disowned, most, but jones

to be, as well, pure warm form,
placental, revolutionary, canonized, and *in it*

which mainly depends on download speed, not distribution.

No money left for space opera,
or cybertherapy, but translating Fanny Howe

into myself demonstrates that
territory and cloud storage

function as relic assumptions betwixt the conjoined.
Tongues. This must be why I bought

the paddleboard and then put it down
in the basement. The ocean is the horizon

as is the sky, none of it when it is!
and Fukishima filling it all in.

I stood on it once, my knees slightly bent,
as a plane roared for Japan,

out of view.

Never stay at an all-inclusive resort undergoing
Brand change if you are reducing
And clammy with 1st
World shame. Rosetta Stone, tip tactically
Immortalize by creating your own weight
In Styrofoam
Better Believe! That nature is cute
And infringing on the backdrops of multiselfies

If the Baja peninsula is really making wine
What is value
ojos de serpiente, el dos de picas

Refugees from the polar vortex come to
San Diego concerned about drought, how
your water isn't enough
In the casino, a rain dance

Google snow glows upon the coast
coats the vagrants on the bridge, angel makers

Each word I looked up each time
It appeared for example planet begat earth
From the dropdown thesaurus

But it lacks precision
In the sense of two finites and what is
The synonym for thesaurus not these choices

Your friends will like that you made a new friend
Between Los Angeles and Tijuana today

But I say, Vacate your position
Atomically, and you'll know what wealth is
You'll have some words

NOTES

The epigraph to this book is from *Crow Versions*, as translated by
W. S. Merwin.

[ey], [bee], and [see] are directly inspired by Charles Bernstein's poem
Fold.

The redacted page-scans in "Pain" are taken from a research contract
between the Office of Naval Research and the University of Florida titled
"Sensory consequences of electromagnetic pulses emitted by laser induced
plasmas." This contract concerns so-called Pulsed Energy Projectiles
(PEPs), which fire a laser pulse that generates a burst of expanding plasma
when it impacts something solid, such as a person, resulting in extreme
though "non-lethal" pain. My thanks to the sadly defunct Sunshine
Project—and to other such entities—for their efforts toward increased
government transparency and accountability. The epigraphs of the poem,
as well as some of the language throughout, are from Thomas Paine,
originally named Pain.

"Google Drive" is a word-by word writing-through of Fanny Howe's
"Robeson Street," from the book of the same title, published in 1985 by
Alice James Books. The line "Schizophrenia is hearing voices, not doing
them" belongs to the comedian Maria Bamford.

ABOUT THE AUTHOR

Ben Doller is the author of *Dead Ahead*, *FAQ:*, and *Radio, Radio*, winner of the Walt Whitman Award. With the poet Sandra Doller, he has published two collaborative books. He is an associate professor of writing and literature at the University of California, San Diego.

A reader's companion is available at http://bendoller.site.wesleyan.edu.